COPPER AND HIS RESCUE FRIENDS

Pam Atherstone

DEDICATION

Rescue is help that gets someone out of a dangerous or unpleasant situation.

A **Volunteer** is someone who does work without being paid for it because they want to do it.

This little book is dedicated to all the **Heroes** known as **Rescuers**, **Fosters**, and **Adopters** and the myriad others who volunteer by cleaning cages, socializing new animals in a rescue, or any other job deemed necessary, as well as those who donate their money to help with veterinary care, food, and whatever else is needed. The Heroes who open their homes, and especially their hearts, to improve the lives of those who provide us with unconditional love.

The dogs and cats (and other companion animals) who only want love and a place to call home but have been neglected, abused, or abandoned through no fault of their own, thank you, too.

THANK YOU

Proceeds from this book will go to local rescues of the author's choice.

TABLE OF CONTENTS

CHAPTER 1

COPPER

Hi! My name is Copper, and I am a rescue dog. That means I was saved by a very kind lady when my previous family didn't want me anymore.

I was born in a warm bed in a lovely house. I had two sisters and four brothers and a very loving Mommy. Our mommy was a Labrador Retriever with short yellow fur. She told us our daddy was an Irish Setter with long red fur and a beautiful boy. All my brothers and sisters were like me, short-furred like Mommy and red like Dad.

One day when I was still very small, a man took me away from my family. He put me in a box with towels on the bottom, and we went for a ride in his car. When we got to his house, he took me out of the box and gave me to the cutest little human I'd ever seen. She had long, curly fur on her head and a sweet smile.

"You must handle your new puppy very gently, Amber. You also need to give him a name," the man said.

"Oh, yes, Daddy. I will! He is so soft, and his fur is the same color as my hair, just like a new penny. I think I will call him Copper."

Amber became my special person. We played together and slept together, and she took me on long walks in the park. She taught me lots of things like how to sit up, how to shake my paw for a treat, and even where I could go potty. Sometimes we just sat in her room, and she would tell me all about her day and her friends and sometimes even her secrets. I loved Amber very much.

When I was about two years old in human years, a day came when Amber didn't want to play with me. She just stayed in bed. I tried to sleep with her, but her Mommy said, "Not today, Copper."

I did my best to make Amber feel better, but she wouldn't get up to play. Then one day, her mommy and daddy took her away. They said they were taking her to someplace called a hospital. I think that's kind of like a veterinarian's office for humans. Anyway, she never came home. Her mommy and daddy cried a lot during this time.

After a time, Amber's parents started shouting at each other. They were never happy, and her mommy would throw things at her daddy. I would hide under Amber's bed for hours, sometimes all night.

One day Amber's daddy put me in the car with my bed and some food. We went for a long ride out to where there were no people or houses. As I looked out the car window, I could see lots and lots of trees in straight rows, but there were no other dogs or other animals that I could see or smell. It was a quiet road.

He finally stopped and got out, and opened my door. "Get out of the car, Copper."

I sat there looking at him because his voice was different somehow.

"Get out, Copper!" he yelled at me this time.

"What did I do wrong? Why are you mad at me?" I wagged my tail. I didn't want to and just sat there looking at him, so he pulled me out by my collar. He put my bed and food in the dirt on the side of the road, then he got back in the car and drove away. I thought he would come back to get me. I sat down on the road and waited and waited. I was so confused and didn't know what to do.

I curled up on my bed when it got dark but didn't sleep. I kept watching for him to come back. It was cold that night, too. I was glad I had my bed to sleep in. The next day I started walking. I thought maybe I could find my way home. I walked and walked until my feet got sore from all the little rocks on the road. Just before the sun went down behind all the trees, I found an old chair beside the road and decided to rest in it for a little while. I slept for the whole night in that ragged old chair.

I woke up the next morning and was very hungry. I remembered the food Amber's daddy left for me, but it was too far to walk back to get it, so I thought I would just keep walking toward home. Maybe someone would find me and help me. I was very sad. But I just kept walking.

I saw a car coming toward me and started to run to it. I didn't recognize this car but hoped it was Amber's daddy. The car got closer and closer, then it slowed down, but it didn't stop.

"Oh, please stop," I sat down on the road and howled. "Please take me home!" The car just kept going. I hung my head down and just sat there. I was too tired and too hungry to keep moving.

I don't know how long it was, but another car came down the road. I didn't have the energy to run for this one, so I just sat there. This car stopped! A lady got out, but it wasn't Amber's mommy.

"Come here, Sweetie." The lady put a bowl on the road and poured some water from a bottle into it. "Are you thirsty?"

I was kind of scared of her but was really thirsty, so I slowly approached the bowl and took a little drink. Then the lady stood up, took a step back, and watched as I drank all the water.

"Such a good boy," she said. "Are you hungry?" She pulled a bag out of her pocket, opened it up, and took something out of it. She squatted down and reached out her hand.

I sniffed the air. "Chicken!" My tail started wagging all on its own. "I love chicken."

"Here you go, big fella," she said as she put some of the chicken in the palm of her hand. I reached out and ate some of that delicious chicken right from her fingers.

She slowly reached out with her other hand and gave me a gentle pet, running her hand down my neck several times and scratching behind my ear. She found my collar and looked at my tag. "You must be lost. Maybe we can find out where you live."

I looked up at her as I licked her fingers, getting the last bit of chicken off them. *If only I could tell her about my family*, I thought.

"Your tag says your name is Copper. Is that right?"

I wagged my tail real fast. "Yes, that's my name," I was excited she knew my name.   "How did you know? I didn't hear my tag say anything. You must be a special human if you can hear things I can't." I gave a happy whine.

"Come on, then, Copper. Let's get you something more to eat while I try to find out where you live." She opened the car door. "Jump in, boy."

The car was smaller than Amber's daddy's car, so it was easy to get into. I immediately smelled other dogs and some strange animals—lots of them. I checked out every spot I could. I wanted to know who these other animals were. I soon found out.

The car went back toward town, but not all the way. The lady talked to me the entire time. Her voice was calming, and I felt comfortable with her. "I sure am glad my friend saw you by the side of the road and called me. Your family will be happy I found you," she said.

The car turned down a road and then into a big yard. The yard was fenced all around, and I could see many other dogs behind the fence. Some barked, some jumped around, and some just waited quietly. As the lady opened the door for me to get out, I heard, "Miss Lily's home!" "Miss Lily, come pet me." "Miss Lily brought us a new friend!" So, now I know the lady's name is Miss Lily.

Miss Lily snapped a leash to my collar before she let me out of the car. "This is so I can protect you from the others, just in case someone gets too rowdy." But I wasn't ready to leave the car. I didn't want to join the others. I wanted Miss Lily to take me to my home.

"Come on, boy. It's okay. They won't bother you."

But I was sad. I wanted Amber. I wanted my own home. I lay down on the car seat. Miss Lily tugged at the leash, but I pulled back. "All right, Copper. If you want to stay here for a while longer, that's okay, too." Miss Lily removed the leash and closed the door. "I'll be back in a few minutes with more food and water for you."

She did come with some food and water. Then she put all the other dogs in the house and came and moved the car inside the fenced yard. She got out and left all the car's doors open, so I could get out to potty if I had to. She let the others back outside, and everyone started doing their own thing, and most paid no attention to me except for one tiny black and brown girl dog. At first, she just put her front feet up on the edge of the doorframe. "Why won't you come to join us? Don't you like us?"

"I don't belong here. I want to go to my home."

"Is Miss Lily taking you there? Is that why you're staying in the car?"

"I hope so," I sighed a big sigh.

"You could still come and play with us while you wait for Miss Lily. She won't mind." Her short stub of a tail wagged really hard. "We have lots of toys, big ones and little ones, and even some in the middle."

"No, I don't feel like playing; I'm worn out from trying to find my family. I'm sad because I miss them. I think I want to sleep now." I got up and turned around to find a comfortable spot on the car seat.

The little dog jumped in the car and onto the seat beside me. "That's fine. I'll sleep, too." She snuggled along my side and yawned. "By the way, my name is Peanut."

I licked her head. "Hello, Peanut; nice to meet you."

I don't know how long we slept before Miss Lily returned to the car. She got in the car and sat next to Peanut and me. "I'm sorry, Copper." Her voice was sad and quiet as she reached out and stroked my back. "I finally got your vet on the phone, and he told me your family has moved away. He told me about Amber and her illness."

My ears perked up, "Amber? Did you find Amber? Is she coming for me? How soon will she be here?" I jumped up and licked Miss Lily's face.

"No, boy," Miss Lily pushed me back. "No, Amber isn't coming; I'm sorry. There is no family for you now. Amber went over the Rainbow Bridge, and her parents split up and left town. I think you reminded them too much of her; that's why they left you behind." Miss Lily sighed and rubbed my head. "I don't understand why people don't at least try to find a new home for their pets. After all, they are family, too. You might as well come into the house and settle in now. Maybe we can find you a new family to love."

I wasn't sure what she was telling me, but I understood her mood. I could feel her sadness. I was very sad, too. I hung my head and still didn't want to leave the car.

Peanut jumped up and put her feet against my neck. "Come on, Copper. Come into the house with us. It's going to get cold out here in the car tonight. I don't like being cold. Come on, Copper."

"Okay, I guess one night won't hurt. It might be nice to have a warm bed."

"Of course it is!" Peanut screeched in her high voice. "You'll like it."

Miss Lily again attached the leash to my collar and led me out of the car. I went with her this time because I didn't want another night out in the cold. She led me to the porch and up the ramp to her house.

As Miss Lily opened the door, Peanut ran past me, barking excitedly. The other dogs got all excited, too, and were going around in all directions. Peanut barked in her screechy voice, "Calm down, everyone. This is Copper. He's been lost, and we need to find him a new home."

There was a lot of tail wagging and sniffing as I entered the door. "Hi, Copper." "Nice to meet you, Copper." "Will you be staying long?" "How'd you get lost?"

"Will you be our friend?" "Can I play with you?" Everyone was talking at the same time.

"Now, everybody, just calm down. Copper needs some rest and time to get to know us." Miss Lily shooed the others away as she led me into the kitchen. "I hope you like cats, Copper, because there are a few in here, and I don't want any trouble."

I looked up at Miss Lily. "What's a cat?" About that time, a strange-looking dog walked up to me and started rubbing against my chest. This dog was all white, with long soft fur. It made a strange noise, kind of like a growl, but not exactly. I didn't feel threatened. It seemed to be happy. It smelled weird, though, like the smells from the car, but not like any dog I've ever smelled before.

"Meow," it said, "my name is Snow. You seem nice. Are you? Do you like cats?"

"Are you a cat?" I asked. "I don't think I've ever met a cat before. Why do you ask if I like cats?"

Snow sat down and licked a paw. "Because a lot of dogs don't. They chase us, try to catch us, and think we are some sort of chew toy. Some dogs even kill cats. Dogs can be very scary for us."

My eyes got very wide. "Dogs do that? They must be the same dogs who fight with other dogs. Some dogs think they are big bullies. I don't know why or what pleasure they get out of being a bully. I am not one of those dogs."

Snow got up and rubbed her body along my side. "I'm happy to hear that, Copper. Welcome to Miss Lily's Rescue."

"What's a rescue?"

A big dog with a curly tan-colored coat came up to us. "Hi, I'm Shaggy. A rescue is where animals go to live when they become lost or sick or are just different enough that they can't find a new home. Miss Lily tries to find homes for some of us, but some of us will live here forever."

"Oh," I said, still not entirely understanding what he meant. "What do you mean by different?"

Shaggy sat down and lifted his front paw toward Snow. "Many of us have things that are not normal. Snow here can't see; she's blind. I have a hip that doesn't work right, and sometimes it hurts a lot. Peanut is missing most of her tail. One of the cats is very old, so most humans won't take him because he needs extra care. There are other problems, too, but if you stay for a while, you'll see what I mean."

"So that's what happened to my Amber? She got sick, and her parents found a rescue for her?"

"Perhaps," Shaggy said. "If that's what happened, then your Amber is probably happy with her new friends."

"But I still don't understand why I couldn't go with her," I felt sad again.

"Maybe because dogs aren't allowed at a human rescue," Shaggy shrugged. "The best thing you can do is try to be happy here with the rest of us. Miss Lily is kind and gives all of us lots of love. If you are a good boy, you'll get toys and treats, too."

"I like toys and treats." I wagged my tail. "I like Miss Lily, too; she's been very nice to me. She found me and brought me here instead of driving past me like the other car did. I guess I'll stay for now."

That was some time ago. I have learned to accept that Amber is never coming back. Although some people came to look at me and take me to their homes, Miss Lily decided I should stay with her. She says I have something called depression, and she just wants me to be happy and loved.

I love Miss Lily and my new family. Most of the others are fun to be with, and everyone has their own story. Most of all, they were rescued just like me!

I like talking to the other animals and learning about their lives before I met them. I hope you enjoy learning about them, too.

CHAPTER 2

OLD JAKE

Since I was new to cats, I thought Old Jake would be an excellent first chat because he seemed pretty mellow and might be more willing to talk to me.

I found him curled up under the couch, watching the other cats romp across the floor. I sat down near him and asked, "Whatcha doing?"

The big orange tabby licked the striped fur along his side. "What's that you say?" he meowed.

"Whatcha doing?" I repeated, a bit louder this time.

Jake shook his head, licked a front paw, and rubbed it over his ear. "I don't hear so well anymore. I'm just watching these young'uns play their silly games, I guess. What are you doing, Copper?"

"I was wondering if you could tell me about you. You know…how you came to live here with Miss Lily."

"I remember hearing a mouse under the grass from the top of a tree in the California heat. We had to be tough back then. You had to be one tough %@#$%@#$%#."

I gasped. "I can't use bad words. It's not nice."

Old Jake snarled, "Listen here, boy…when you get to be 171/2 years old like I am, you can use whatever words you want!"

"Miss Lily!" I cried out, "Old Jake isn't being good."

Miss Lily's voice came from the next room, "JAKE! Use your nice words. We've talked about that."

Jake rolled his eyes and snarled again. "Fine."

"Jake, would you please tell me how you met Miss Lily?"

Jake stared off into the distance. "That was many moons ago. Back when I was a wee one."

My eyes got huge, and my mouth popped open, "You mean you used to be little?"

"Everyone used to be little. I was smaller than Miss Lily's hand. I was teeny tiny."

"Wow.... that's hard to imagine."

Jake got up, stretched, then sat up and faced me, "Make yourself comfortable, tail-wagger, and I'll tell you my story about how I met Miss Lily."

"Yes, sir." I circled around and lay down on the floor in front of Jake.

"Good boy. Now, where do I begin?" Jake looked up, deep in thought. "My very first memory is of me walking through the fence. I was so tiny that all I had to do was turn my head sideways, and through it, I went."

"Whaaaaat? That means you were smaller than my paw." I couldn't believe big Old Jake was ever that tiny.

"That's right, I was and barely had any teeth. I had to have a special diet with canned milk and rice… it was creamy and oh so delicious."

Now I was drooling because I love milk and rice. "Oh, that does sound yummy. Okay, okay. So, how did you meet Miss Lily?"

"Oh yes, yes. I get sidetracked a lot these days. Back in the day, I used to have focus. I would lay out in the soft grass catching birds all day. I remember this one time when a hawk almost got me; that cost me some fur. Miss Lily stopped letting anyone under a certain size outside after that."

I exasperatedly put my paw across my muzzle, "Jake, that does sound scary, but how did you meet Miss Lily?"

"Oh yes, yes... After walking through the fence, I ran the best I could to the porch and then had to climb up the giant steps. I was so little it felt near impossible, but I was determined, and with every ounce that my tiny self had, I made it to the top."

I shook my head, "Wait. Wait. Jake, we don't have steps."

Jake laughed, "Oh, you, silly tail-wagger. This was before Miss Lily had the ramps installed. She did that when Bernie, our chocolate Lab who lived here back then, started having trouble walking."

"Oh, okay. Bernie? Wait, let's not get sidetracked again."

"Remember, boy, this was back when everything was bigger, life was harder, and we had to be tougher. The dogs were meaner, the cats were craftier, and catnip was just catnip, not that fancy stuff these cats get nowadays. And our only toys were paper balls made from Miss Lily's junk mail."

I was shocked. "No way..."

16

Jake looked down at his feet, "We didn't have as much as you spoiled tail-waggers have nowadays."

I shook my head to try and clear my thoughts. "Wait. Wait. We're getting off track again. How did you meet Miss Lily?"

"Yes, yes. I was getting to that. So, after that long trip across the yard and up the steps, I found the dog door."

In disbelief, I tilted my head to one side, "The dogs had their own door?"

Jake threw his head back and laughed, "No, boy. That's just what it was called; everyone could use it... IF... they were big enough to push the flappy thing open, kinda like the ones on the big dog house out in the front yard."

I laughed and nodded my understanding, "Got it."

Jake continued," So when I got to the door, I was too little to get it to move. I tried and tried, but I gave up and started screaming at the door. The next thing I know, the big door came open real fast, and a young woman stepped out."

I interrupted, "A young woman? Who was it?"

Jake put his paw on his forehead and sighed, "Really, Copper?"

I was confused, "What?" I asked.

Jake shook his head in disgust, "It was Miss Lily, Copper."

"Oooooh... I guess that makes sense."

Jake rolled his eyes, "Yes, Copper. Everyone used to be young, even Miss Lily."

"Okay, sorry. I never really thought about it. So, what happened when she came out?"

"Well, first off, I thought I would get hit by the door; it had opened so fast. But I didn't. I let out a loud shriek, and that's when she saw me and scooped me up. She took me inside and kissed me on the forehead. She talked nicely to me and loved on me a bit while she looked me all over, making sure I wasn't hurt or anything. Then she made me some yummy creamy food." Jake stopped for a minute and stared into the distance. "I still remember that first bit of goodness hitting the empty spot in my tummy." Jake looked up at me and continued, "That Copper, my boy, is how I met Miss Lily."

"Wow, that's a good story." I was amazed at how gentle Miss Lily must have been with such a tiny fur ball.

Jake got up and walked toward his bed in the cat room, "I suppose it is. I've been around a long time; I've seen a lot of things, and I've seen so many others come and go. Miss Lily says I'm so old that I can do whatever I want."

Miss Lily came into the room, "ALMOST whatever you want."

Jake rolled his eyes, "Fine. Almost whatever I want."

I licked the old cat's head, "Thank you for sharing your story with me."

Jake stopped and turned back toward me, "It was fun. Most tail-waggers don't sit and listen as well as you.

If you'd like to do this again, I have many stories, but I'm tired and need a nap now. Goodnight, Copper."

"Goodnight, Jake."

I had so much fun listening to Old Jake. I can't wait to do it again. I never realized how much our elders could know and that it was more challenging back then than it is now. I have gained a new appreciation for what I have. I highly recommend talking to your elders. Spread some love and share some cheer. Remember, every day can be a new beginning.

CHAPTER 3

SHAGGY

I decided to talk to my mellow buddy Shaggy. He is also known to my human friends as "The Hug Dog" because he loves to hug, and everybody loves to hug him back because he's so big and, well…shaggy.

Shaggy and I were lying in the sun, enjoying the soft breeze ruffling through our fur. I rolled over on my back to let the sun warm my belly. "Hey, Shaggy."

Shaggy rolled on his side, letting the sun's warmth shine on his bad hip. "What, buddy?"

I turned my head in his direction, "Can I ask you something?"

Shaggy chuckled, "Let me guess. You want to know my story."

I gazed up at the clouds, "Yeah."

Shaggy closed his eyes, deep in thought. "When I was a pup, I was put into a cardboard box with my siblings and taken to a place where there were lots of people and cars and those wheely carts humans put their food in at the stores. It was a hot day, and there was no water or food for us. One by one, my siblings were taken by people walking by, and I was the last one in the box at the end of the day. I was so hot and thirsty that I just curled up in the corner of the box and tried to pretend I wasn't there. Finally, a man came and looked at me and picked me up. He was gentle and spoke to me in a soft voice. I tried to wag my tail, but I was just too miserable. He talked to the human who had me in the box, then held me up and said, "Would you like to come with me?' I licked him on his hairy chin, and he laughed. I learned his name was Ernie."

I put my head on my paws. "What then?"

"Ernie carried a sack on his back. He reached into it and pulled out a bottle with some water in it and a small dish. He set me on the ground, poured the water into the dish, and gave me a drink. I drank and drank until my belly was full. Ernie also had a wheely cart, but his had a lot of stuff in it."

I raised my head in curiosity, "What kind of stuff?"

Shaggy opened his eyes, and I could see how much he missed this Ernie person. "Almost everything he needed. There were blankets and towels and clothes and a cooking pot. He also picked up things as he walked around the neighborhood, like scraps of metal, an old broom with no handle, and empty bottles and cans. Just stuff."

Shaggy put his head on his paws. "He pulled out a blanket, put it on top of his stuff, and put me on top. Then he pushed me in his cart to a place where there was grass everywhere and lots of big trees. When he found a spot he liked, he put me on the grass to rest, pulled out his blankets, and told me we were going to sleep there. He shared a bit of bread and meat with me, too."

"You got to sleep outside in the grass under the trees? Gosh, isn't that every dog's dream?" I asked.

"It wasn't a bad life for me. Ernie was a great guy. He looked after me as best as he could, even if he didn't have a real house or anything. He always shared what food he had with me, and I protected him when he needed me to. Once I got big enough to keep up with him, we walked all over the city. We spent warm nights in places with grass and trees, and on cold or rainy nights, he would find covered spaces by buildings. I would snuggle up to him, and we kept each other warm." Shaggy let out a big sigh.

"So, if you had such a great human and a good life, how did you get here?" I was kind of confused.

"Ernie and I were together for about four years. I never left him, and he never left me. Then one morning, Ernie didn't wake up. I tried and tried to get him to move, but he wouldn't. I even grabbed his arm in my mouth and tried to make him get up. Then I thought he might need human help, so I sat beside him and howled until someone came. That person tried to get Ernie to wake up, too, but even they couldn't do it.

"Soon, a big white van with a loud howl and bright flashing lights came. Two men got out and yelled at me to get away. They put Ernie on a bed and put him in the van. That was the last time I saw him." Shaggy sniffled and sighed again. I think he was trying not to cry.

"Then what happened?"

Shaggy looked up and watched the clouds pass by. "Well… I lived on my own for a while. It's rough being on your own. Food is hard to find, and sometimes you have to fight others for survival. It's really hard."

I shook my head, "That does sound rough. I didn't think you'd ever been in a fight; you're always so chill and kind. You don't even bark at stuff."

Shaggy looked over at me, "I didn't like it, but I did what I had to do. I wandered our old neighborhoods hoping someone would recognize me as being Ernie's dog and maybe take me in, but nobody did. I finally found a house I liked because the people there had given Ernie and me some food one time. I hoped they would remember me, so I waited by the gate, just sitting patiently. I was hungry, and part of the right side of my face was swollen and hanging."

My eyes got huge with shock. "Wait! What?"

Shaggy continued, "I got hurt really bad in a fight."

I shook my head and rolled over to join him in the cloud- watching, "That's horrible."

Shaggy took a deep breath, "It was. I waited by the gate until I finally saw car lights, and my tail started wagging. I knew this had to be someone who would take me in, so I ran out to greet them. Suddenly, something big hit me. It knocked me out into the street, and I rolled over and over. I just knew this was it. It was over. I was done."

My eyes locked on Shaggy, "That's awful!"

Shaggy blinked, stood up, stretched, and sat down, "Yeah, it was. It was very dark that night and cold. Well, I tried to get up and run, but my back leg hurt so bad it wouldn't let me get up. I heard yelling, and the next thing I knew, someone threw a blanket over me, picked me up, and put me in their car. I was weak and tired, and scared. The ride didn't take long, but I felt so much pain that it seemed like forever. When we stopped, the man who was driving carried me into a building like I'd never been in before. It was bright, and there were people and other dogs sitting in the room. The man who carried me was quickly taken into a separate room, and I was laid on a cold metal table. Another man came in and said he was Doctor Mike. He examined me, touched me gently, and said I had a broken hip and needed my face treated. I also needed medicine and food.

I don't remember much after that. I guess I was so tired that I went to sleep. When I woke up, I was in a cage. There were other cages with dogs and cats in them, too. I was confused and still in pain, but not as much as the night before. Dr. Mike came in and checked on me and told me he had fixed my hip, but I would have to stay calm and not try to stand up. He gave me some soft food and a little water. I slept a lot. I guess because there was nothing else to do in that cage. I don't know how long I was there, but I watched most of the other dogs and cats go home, and new ones came in, and then they went home, too. Finally, Dr. Mike came and said I was going home with someone special who would take good care of me."

"Miss Lily?" I asked, but I knew that's who it was; it just had to be.

Shaggy grinned, "You are right. The first thing she did was open my cage, and she hugged me and told me she would love me. Dr. Mike carried me out to her car, and she drove me here. She put me in a special pen where no one could bother me. She brought medicine and soft food and sat and fed me."

I tilted my head, a bit confused. "Why was she feeding you?"

"My face was still swollen from the fight and hurt too much to eat on my own. After I ate and took the medicine, she turned the garden into a kennel with a little house just for me so I could recover without getting excited or too active. It took a long time for me to heal. Miss Lily would come out and hug me and bring medicine and all the food I could eat. Finally, I got better and could play with the other dogs. But, as I get older, my hip hurts again. It aches when I run too much or when the weather gets cold, which is why I limp and lay in the sun so much. So, I just chill and enjoy my life. I appreciate how lucky I am and the family I have."

I sat quietly, speechless for a moment, "That is truly an amazing story. Thank you for sharing."

Shaggy got up and shook the dry grass from his fur. He turned and started to walk away, then looked over his shoulder back at me, "I have learned never to take who or what I have in life for granted and to enjoy the little things, even if it's just for a fleeting moment."

I lay back down and rolled over to watch the clouds again as I thought about what Shaggy just told me. I had no idea Shaggy had been through so much. I will make sure I appreciate everyone and everything that I have. I think everyone should. We may not have a lot, but Shaggy is right about appreciating the little things. Oh, and if you put a bunch of little things together, they might make a big thing.

CHAPTER 4

SNOW

I walked into the living room one afternoon, and Snow was stretched out on the back of the couch, dozing in the sunlight streaming through the big window. I tried to be quiet as I passed by, but she raised her head and sniffed the air.

"Where are you going, Copper?"

"Outside," I said. "Wait, how did you know it was me?"

Snow smiled a sly kitty smile. "I have my ways," she purred.

I stopped in my tracks and turned toward her as she hopped down onto the couch cushion, her long white fur flowing around her. She sat in the middle of the cushion and licked her fur smooth along her back.

"What do you mean by that?" I asked.

"Just because I can't see doesn't mean I don't know what's happening around me."

Now I was kind of curious but also a bit afraid. Although Snow was the first cat I had ever met, and she treated me kindly, the fact that she could not see troubled me. I wasn't sure why. I was always cautious around her; I sure didn't want to cause her any harm by stepping on her accidentally or running into her without warning. "Will you tell me how you knew it was me?"

"I'd be happy to. Come up here next to me so we can cat-chat." Snow curled up on the cushion as I jumped up and sat in the far corner of the couch. "Don't be so distant. Come closer; I won't bite." She sounded almost disappointed in me, so I made myself get close to her and lay next to her. She put her paw on my paw. "See? Is this so bad?"

"No, Snow. Actually, it's kind of nice. Your fur is so soft."

Snow smiled again. "Now, about how I know what's around me," she began. "I was born without the ability to see, but I can still smell, feel, hear, and taste, just like all the other animals around here. I have learned that each one of you has a different smell. Also, everyone sounds different when they walk across the floor. You are a big boy, so you take longer between steps than Peanut does. Old Jake moves slowly; Shaggy has a bad hip, so he kind of drags his back foot a little; Shadow has extra big feet, so she makes a little thud when she walks."

"Wow, I never knew all of that." I tilted my head as I tried to "listen" to the other animals, even though they were all out of the room at the moment.

Snow laughed, "You will catch on if you pay attention."

"So, how can you move around the house without running into things?" This was something I'd watched her do, and she always made it through the room without crashing.

"That's a little different but kind of the same. First, Miss Lily is very good at not moving things around too much. So, I have formed a kind of…Ummm…map in my brain. I guess you could call it that. Since I have never seen things and don't know what they look like, I have made my own picture in my mind. Miss Lily has told me what table and chair legs are. I "see" them as narrow barriers, smooth all around and smelling sort of like a tree. I know the room where Miss Lily eats has lots of these barriers, so when I go in there, I walk slowly and use my nose and whiskers to find my way through. I usually only go there when Miss Lily is eating because she sometimes gives me little treats."

"Why do you use your whiskers?" I know cats have long whiskers, but I didn't know they could be used for things. My whiskers are just fancy decorations, although now that I think about it, I can sense a few things with them.

Snow turned her head to one side. "Can you see them? Are they longer than yours?"

"I think so," I responded as I tried to look down my nose to see my own.

"My whiskers are very sensitive. I can tell how big something is, whether it is hot or cold, how far away it is, and whether there is enough space for me to get past it. The other cats have told me they can even tell which way the wind is blowing, but Miss Lily never lets me go outside, so I haven't needed them for that. Watch this."

Snow thrust her whiskers forward. "This means I'm alert or curious about something." Then her whiskers were pulled back and flattened against her face. "This means I might be scared or angry, and you'd better watch out!" She shook her head, and her whiskers stuck straight out to the sides. "Now, I'm happy and relaxed," she smiled and lay her head back on her paws.

"Wow, that's so cool. I never knew that. Do all cats do that or only blind ones?"

"All cats can do that. Watch the other cats, and you will see and be able to tell how they feel."

"So, if Killer Klaws…I mean, Shadow…is in a bad mood; I can tell before I get close to her."

"Exactly."

"What other things can you do?" I was interested in knowing more about Snow's abilities.

"I don't think I do anything special. I think I pay more attention to other things because I can't see. Like hearing. I told you how I could tell who is in the room by the sounds they make when they walk. Everyone is different in some way, and I have just learned who makes what sounds and how they make those sounds. Just like my toys. Miss Lily gives me toys that make noise. Some have little bells; some make crinkly noises, and some squeak like a mouse. I can bat them around the room and still find them."

I thought about all the cat toys around the house, and it seemed they all make some kind of noise. "How do you know your toys from the other cats' toys?"

Snow thought for a minute. "Maybe cats can do something else dogs can't do."

"What's that?"

"We leave smells on things with our feet."

"How do you do that?" I was really interested now.

"We have little glands on the pads of our feet that leave a scent when we walk or touch something. I know my own scent and can follow it to find where I've been before and know it is safe to walk there. I can also tell when a toy belongs to one of the other cats and which cat it is."

"Oh, I understand smell. We dogs are always smelling things and can tell a whole lot about other dogs, other animals, or even humans by the smells they leave behind. I guess cats have their own way of smelling these things."

Snow rolled over on her back between my front paws. She reached up and placed her fluffy white paw against my nose. "I think you are starting to understand that cats are different from dogs, and just because I can't see, I'm not all that different from the other cats."

I licked Snow on the chin, "I guess we're all different in some way. I know now that there is nothing to be afraid of just because someone is different; they have to be themselves to get by in this world. Miss Lily says she loves us so much because we are all different. Maybe everyone would be happier if they only understood their differences and loved each other for who they are."

"You're a good boy Copper. You do try to understand," Snow purred.

I lay my head next to hers, and we both took a long nap.

CHAPTER 5

SHADOW

Today I decided to visit Shadow. None of the other rescues call her that because Shadow is one terrifying black cat. She hates dogs and has super big paws with extra toes, so when she takes a swipe at you with her claws out, it hurts! The other animals call her Killer Klaws, but I don't like calling her names because that's not nice.

Shadow sleeps in a unique room with bars all around. Miss Lily calls it a crate and says it protects Shadow from the rest of us. Really? We all need protection from Shadow!

I sat outside the door of the big room where all the cats sleep. Shadow was in her crate. I took a deep breath before entering and told myself, *you can do this. You're not scared. You are a good boy. Go for it.*

As I walked through the doorway into the cat room, I saw Old Jake curled up on top of his cat condo. He opened one eye and watched me as I walked toward Shadow. She glared at me through the bars of her room and hissed, "Hello, precious, ready to meet your maker?"

I sat down just out of her reach, "No, Ma'am, I just came to talk."

Shadow's green eyes got enormous and scary. She reached one of her giant paws through the bars and tried to slap my nose. "With me?" she laughed gruesomely, making the fur on my back twitch.

I swallowed hard and dropped my head. "I just wanted to learn about you."

Shadow stood up, arched her back, turned her tail to me, and said, "Go on, I'm intrigued."

"Well, I was wondering why you attack us dogs?"

Shadow laughed her scary laugh again, then jumped against the bars of her crate, "Because I'm craaaaazzy!"

Old Jake lifted his head and yawned. "Copper, why are you talking to her? She certainly is crazy; she's the craziest cat I've ever met."

"Well, sir, I just wanted to know why she is so mean to us dogs."

Shadow kept laughing as Old Jake slowly shook his head. "Maybe you should start with her kitten years and work up to that."

I nodded my head, "Yes, sir. An excellent idea."

Shadow stopped laughing and faced me with a quiet growl.

With Old Jake close by, I was less scared. "Umm, Shadow, I was wondering ..."

"I'll tell you anything for a chunk of your nose."

My eyes got big, and I covered my nose with my paw.

Old Jake hissed at Shadow, "Stop tormenting the tail wagger and tell him your story."

39

Shadow gave Old Jake a side eye, "You're no fun, old man."

"Yes, you're right. I am so old your words don't bother me. Now be nice and tell him your story," Jake grumbled.

Shadow punched her blanket with her big front feet, "Okay, I guess I'll be nice."

I moved a little closer to Shadow's room. "I was told when Miss Lily brought you to live here, you had trouble walking, and your head shook."

Shadow looked down at her feet. "I was born in a pile of old weeds, along with two sisters and a brother. My momma didn't have a home. We had to hunt and find our own food. One day I got my head stuck in something called a plastic cup. I could hardly walk, or eat, or drink water. My momma tried to remove that thing from my head, but when she couldn't, she left me under an old house. She needed to hunt to feed the others. I spent days in that thing, and it started cutting into my neck."

My mouth dropped open, "How awful. Did your mommy come back? How did you get out of it?"

"Mommy came back a couple of times. She even brought me a mouse to eat. But I couldn't get close enough to it to get it in my mouth. I could only sit and cry. Then one day, a girl came and found me."

"Miss Lily?" my eyes brightened.

"No, she was called Mindy. I tried to run away, but it's hard to run with a cup on your head. She caught me and took me to her house, and her daddy cut the cup off me. They were very nice at first. But then Mindy's daddy started working out of town and left Mindy to care for me. That's when my head started shaking all the time, and I couldn't walk very well. Mindy was supposed to work with me and help me walk and stuff. But she always had something else to do, and I was forgotten."

"I'm sorry." I stared down at my front paws. "That is so sad."

Shadow ruffled her blanket a bit and snuggled down into it. "Then, one day, my skin had strange gooey spots. They itched and turned red. Mindy didn't know what to do, so she called Miss Lily. She heard about Miss Lily from a friend. Anyway, Miss Lily thought she could help me, so she took me to a vet. The vet was nice and examined me all over. The vet said I was allergic to fleas, and I had brain damage from the cup pinching the nerves in my neck."

"And then you came here?"

"Not yet," Shadow said. "The vet gave Miss Lily some medicine for the sores and some vitamins for the rest of me. Miss Lily took me back to Mindy and told her how to care for me. Miss Lily checked on me the next week and discovered that Mindy was not giving me the medicine. Mindy wasn't helping me with my walking, either."

I just sat there feeling Shadow's misery.

Shadow continued her story. "Miss Lily decided right then to bring me here. After about a week with Miss Lily, my skin was clear, and my walking was much better. Miss Lily made me my special room and found me a different doctor. She bought some rubbery floor mats to help me walk on the slippery floors. It took a long time and lots of help from Miss Lily, but I can run and jump and play, just not as gracefully as the other cats."

I tilted my head as I looked at her, still a bit confused. "But that doesn't explain why you are mean to us dogs. Or why everyone calls you Killer Klaws."

Shadow's piercing eyes widened, and her pupils tightened into narrow slits. "Because you all step on me," she hissed. "I can't get out of the way as quickly as the others. My only defense is to be mean and swipe at you with my big paws and extra claws. If I'm mean, maybe you will keep your distance."

I looked at my feet, picked up my front paw, and looked it over. "I try to be careful."

Shadow shrugged. "Not enough!" she meowed loudly. "I have enough issues without being stepped on."

It hurt my feelings when she said that, but I understood. Shadow rose from her blanket and turned around, and lay down facing away from me. Old Jake lay with his head on his front paws watching from his perch. "Copper, don't let her get to you. As much as you try, you can't make everyone your friend."

I looked up at Jake with a disappointed look on my face.

Jake raised his head and looked at me thoughtfully. "You're a good boy, Copper. That's just how life is. The important thing is always to be considerate of others and not let them get you down. You be you."

I stared at Old Jake for a minute letting his words sink into my brain. "Okay, I will try very hard." I looked at Shadow sleeping in her crate and sighed, "I think it's time for me to go back outside now."

I stepped out of the cat's room and sat silently in the hallway. My visit didn't go quite as I thought it would. Shadow may not want to be my friend, but I won't let that stop me from being who I am. I will continue to spread as much love and kindness as I can. I will be more aware of Shadow when she is among the rest of us; just because she doesn't want to be my friend doesn't mean I can't still love and be kind to her. Maybe someday she'll change her mind.

CHAPTER 6

BELLA BEAGLE

I got a lesson in understanding this week. I never realized how important understanding was; this is how my lesson happened.

Miss Lily and I were sitting on the porch ramp, and I was telling her about how mean and selfish Bella Beagle is and how I don't think she should be mean and selfish because I'm not mean or selfish, and I can't think of any reason to be mean or selfish.

Miss Lily put her hand on my head and said, "It's not fair to judge someone before spending a day in their fur."

"What does that mean?" I asked

Miss Lily smiled at me. "It means you should try to understand where someone comes from and what they've been through or are going through before you form an opinion about them." Miss Lily looked up toward the sky and thought for a moment, then looked at me and said, "Maybe it would be a good idea to talk with Bella. That might give you a better understanding of why she is who she is."

Miss Lily has the best ideas. Now, I'm off to talk to Bella, the hoarder of the dog bowls, the claimer of the doghouse, the queen of the nervous. I'm going to see if I can find out why she is like she is.

I walked down the ramp as Miss Lily went back into the house. I looked for Bella but didn't see her anywhere, so I quietly went over to the doghouse. I hoped Bella wasn't taking a nap because she isn't fun if you wake her up. So, I tried to be as quiet as possible as I stuck my head into the doghouse to see if she was awake.

"GET OUT OF MY DOGHOUSE!"

I jumped back because she scared me. "Miss Lily says you're supposed to share."

Bella was harsh and irritated, "I don't care," she growled.

I barked, "Miss Lily! Miss Lily! Bella won't share!"

Miss Lily came out of the house and stood on the porch. She saw Bella and me standing nose to nose in the door of the doghouse. "Bella, be nice," she said sternly.

Bella slowly stepped out of the doghouse, stretching with every step, "Okay," she answered in a deep growl.

Miss Lily turned to go back inside the house, glancing over her shoulder at Bella.

Bella sneered and gave me the side-eye, "You just had to go and tell on me."

I hung my head, a little bit embarrassed at being a tattle-tale, "Sorry, but you are supposed to share; that is our doghouse. Right, Shaggy?"

Shaggy was lying in the grass nearby. His eyes widened, and he shook his head, "Pick your battles, boy.

I don't want any part of that. Plus, I heard Miss Lily's going to build us another doghouse. Just let Bella have it. You rarely want to sleep in it anyways."

I sat down, "Yes, maybe you're right."

Bella sat down and looked up at the sun, then threw herself on the ground and started scratching her back in the grass and pawing in the air. "So, Copper. Why did you risk waking me up?"

I stood up, walked over, and sat beside Bella, "I wanted to ask you about where you came from."

Bella stopped and rolled over. She looked me straight in the eyes, "Why?"

I opened my eyes wide; her reaction was so powerful, "Uuuhhhh...because I know very little about you. You spend most of your time alone, and you never want to share. Did I do something to make you not want to share with me? I'm sorry I'm so big, and I stepped on you once. It was an accident."

Bella's eyes softened, "Oh, Copper. You have nothing to apologize for. I like you just the way you are. You didn't do anything wrong to me. I don't even remember you stepping on me, and I know that if you did, it was certainly an accident. You're a good boy."

I wagged my tail; it was nice to hear her being nice.

Bella got up and sat right next to me, "I guess I could give you a little information about me."

I gave her a big doggy grin, "I would appreciate that. Can I share your experience with the others?"

Bella tilted her head to one side, thinking about my question. "I guess that would be okay. I know you love them, and you like keeping everyone happy."

My tail started thumping on the grass as Bella looked down at her paws, "I wish I knew them when I was little. Let me tell you what Miss Lily rescued me from."

I could see the pain on Bella's face, so I put my paw on hers. She looked up with sad eyes. "You really are a good boy." Bella cleared her throat and straightened her back, "So, when I was little, I lived in a yard with lots of other dogs and puppies. Our humans didn't live there, but they would drive by once a week and throw nasty dog food over the fence. It was always in a big sack that would break open when it landed on the ground. If any of us pups were in the way, we could be squished, so we all ran away from the fence when we saw that car coming. Then because I was so little, my mommy would have to fight for food to bring to me while I stayed hidden."

My mouth dropped open with anger, "That's awful!"

"Yes, it was. Then some kids started jumping over the fence so they could chase us with sticks and be mean to us."

I shook my head slowly, "That's scary. What did you do?"

Tears formed in the corners of Bella's eyes, "The only thing I could do...I ran and hid. I learned to be scared of people and to run when I saw one. Then, I would start shaking, hoping they wouldn't find me. My mommy would do her best to keep them away from me. She would snarl and growl at them. She even tried to bite one of them, but they used their sticks to keep her away."

I licked her tears as they streamed down her face, "I'm so sorry that happened to you. That must have been extremely scary and tough."

Bella took a deep breath, "Then, one day, a woman and two big guys showed up. I went to run and hide, but one guy came up behind me while the other stood in front of me. I started yelping, and I didn't know where my mommy was. Those guys started chasing me. I was screaming. Then I heard the woman yell at the guys, and everything seemed to stop. It was like the whole world got quiet. The woman walked right up to me and scooped me up. I yelped out of fear; then, I piddled all over her. I started to shake all over; I just knew whoever this was who was holding me would be mad and mean, but she wasn't. She kissed my forehead and carried me to her truck."

I interrupted Bella with my excitement, "It was Miss Lily!"

Bella laughed, "Yes, Copper, it was Miss Lily. I was such a pain in the tail when she brought me home. Everything and everyone were so big and new; I was so frightened. Whenever anything or anyone touched me, I would scream and piddle out of fear. It was so embarrassing."

I tilted my head and asked, "Piddle?"

"You know," Bella leaned toward me and whispered, "I peed."

I looked at her with kindness, "That does sound embarrassing. How did you get through it?"

Bella smiled at me. "Miss Lily, of course. My first night was very upsetting and comforting at the same time. That was when I realized I might actually be okay. It was about bedtime, and Miss Lily let everyone out to potty before bed. I didn't want to go. I tried to hide under the coffee table, but I think the wet trail gave me away. I didn't think that I should have to go. I mean, I did just piddle all over everything. Why go outside? Anyway, Miss Lily picked me up, and of course, I screamed and piddled on her again. She told me I had to go outside before bed to make good habits."

I smiled: "Miss Lily's all about good habits. My favorite good habit is breakfast. She says it's good for your brain and gives you energy for the day."

Bella nodded, "My favorite good habit is check-in, so Miss Lily can see that we're good and healthy, and if we're not, get us to the doctor if necessary."

My eyes got big with amazement, "That's a good one! I like that one, too."

Bella laughed out loud, "Copper, you like everything." Bella stopped for a minute, deep in thought. "Okay, okay... Where was I? Oh yes, Miss Lily took me outside and placed me on the soft grass. I just sat there terrified, not moving. Then she turned away for half a second, and I scurried under the ramp. I thought no one would be able to find me under there."

"Miss Lily can find anybody," I laughed. "So, did she scoop you up and take you inside?"

Bella took a deep breath, "It wasn't that simple. I had crammed myself into the smallest part at the end of the ramp, where no one could reach."

"Oh no! Did you get stuck?"

"No, but she couldn't get more than fingertips on me. She tried all kinds of snacks and food to bribe me, but I wasn't having it. She even tried canned cat food."

I was shocked, "And you didn't come out?"

Bella shook her head, "Nope, fear is a power that can be stronger than canned cat food...if you let it. Miss Lily lay on the ground with her fingertips on me for a long time, telling me it would be okay. I'm sure she could feel me shaking. Then she got up. I thought she finally decided to give up on me."

I shook my head, "Not our Miss Lily."

Bella continued, "Certainly not. She returned a few minutes later with the thing she uses to lift up the truck."

I gave her a doggy grin, "Miss Lily calls it a two-ton jack. She says it's to lift trucks that have elephants inside. I don't know why anyone would keep an elephant in their truck."

Bella giggled, "She was probably joking when she told you that. Anyway, that's what she used to lift the ramp to get me. When she picked me up, I screamed and piddled on her one last time; she hugged me, kissed my forehead, and told me it was time for bed and that she loved me. After that, I knew I would be safe when she was around."

I sat with a doggy grin and thought momentarily, then looked at Bella, "So, that's why you stash away the food bowls and spend so much time in the doghouse?"

Bella nodded, "Yes. I like to wrestle and play with the toys, but when the rest of you start playing chase, I get scared and freak out and run away to my safe space."

"I'm so sorry, Bella."

Bella had a confused look on her face, "For what?"

I hung my head in shame, "I misjudged you. I should've talked to you instead."

Bella smiled at me, "It's okay. I'm glad we had this talk. It feels good to talk about it. None of the other dogs has ever asked; they keep their distance."

Shaggy had been lying in the grass listening the whole time. He rolled over and sat up as Bella walked back into the dog house, "Copper, I hope you learned something from your talk. I know I did. I'll be nicer to Bella, too."

So, it was a big lesson for me. I learned how understanding is super important. Something I never knew before, but I do now. I think we should all practice understanding. Miss Lily says it would help spread love around the world if we just talked to each other and got to know each other instead of assuming and judging.

CHAPTER 7

ADMIRAL

Shaggy and I were sitting on the back porch one warm afternoon. "I sure would like to talk to Admiral, but he's so serious." I sighed as I leaned against Shaggy.

Admiral is a German Shepherd with fur as dark as night. I don't know why he's called German Shephard because I don't think he was born in Germany, and I've never seen him herding any sheep. Instead, he's always serious-minded and doesn't play around like the rest of us.

Shaggy kept watching Admiral as he patrolled the fence line around the entire yard, always on the lookout. "I'm never sure what he's looking out for, but he's always looking. I heard Miss Lily say he is an OPD."

"What's that?" I asked.

"I'm not sure, but I think it means Overly Patrolling Dog."

Admiral checked the entire yard twice before noticing we were watching him. Finally, he came marching up to us and looked me up and down.

"Why are you just sitting there? There's patrolling to be done." His voice was low and harsh.

I looked at him curiously, "Didn't you just do that?"

Admiral narrowed his dark eyes and looked over his shoulder, "Patrolling never stops. Gotta keep everything safe all the time."

"Are you sure you can't take a break? I wanted to talk to you."

Admiral wrinkled his forehead, "Talk? About what and for how long?"

I swallowed hard, and my body started to shake a little, "I wanted to hear your story about how you met Miss Lily."

Admiral snorted, "I don't think I have that much time." He turned and started to walk off.

Shaggy cleared his throat, "Hey, don't go anywhere. I'll patrol. You talk to Copper."

Admiral grumbled under his breath and gave Shaggy a disgusted glance.

"It won't be that bad. I've got this. You need to chill," Shaggy chuckled.

"Fine!" Admiral snarled.

Shaggy turned and walked off to patrol as I cleared my throat and tried to gather my courage. I wasn't sure why I was so scared of him, he isn't much larger than I am, but he was so intense. "So, how did you meet Miss Lily?"

Admiral sat down and looked over his shoulder, making sure Shaggy was patrolling. "Well, I didn't have an easy start. As a young pup, I was sent to a place where dogs are trained to be guard dogs. It wasn't a bad place;

it was a lot of work and learning to follow orders. But I was more comfortable patrolling and looking for bad guys than I was protecting my human. So, I was sent to a place where I could patrol all day. It was a big place with fences all around the border and hard cement on the ground. Buildings were placed inside the fences, and only a few people came there. Then one day, a big truck came, and the people in the truck started loading things from inside the buildings. Usually, when strangers came into the fenced area, and they were okay to be there, I would be put in my cage. But, this time, no one did that, so I started barking and went after one of the men like I was trained to do. I sunk my teeth into his leg."

"Wow! Did they stop taking stuff?"

"Don't interrupt me. I need to get back to patrolling, and if you interrupt me, it'll take longer to tell my story." Admiral looked out toward the back of the yard where Shaggy was moving along the fence.

I looked down, "Yes, sir, I'm sorry."

Admiral began again, "When I bit that guy, another kicked me so hard I tumbled nose over tail, sprawling across the ground. When I got up and started to run at them again, I heard a loud crack and felt a burning in my shoulder. Then three more men came running up to me and started beating me on my neck and back. I started to run, just as my human caretaker arrived with a bunch of other guys. They started yelling and had their guns out. They caught the bad guys and took them away. I was bleeding and too weak to walk, so my care-taker took me to the veterinarian. The doctor removed a chunk of metal from my shoulder and sewed up my wound. I was so sore that I could hardly walk for a long time. Then after lots of special exercises, I got stronger. But when I returned to work, I couldn't eat or sleep. I just kept patrolling. I wasn't going to let anyone back into the yard. I was taken back to the vet, and he said I could not return to my job."

Shaggy was passing by on one of his rounds and paused, "May I add something?"

Admiral groaned, "Make it quick, then back to patrolling."

Shaggy shook his head, "Calm down; everything is fine." Shaggy looked straight at me with a grin, "That was the morning Miss Lily took me in for an ear infection. Dr. Mike came to Miss Lily and asked if she had room for another special-needs dog. Miss Lily, of course, said yes, and Admiral came home with us that very day."

Admiral let out a big breath, "Are you finished?"

Shaggy stuck his tongue out at Admiral, rocked his head mockingly, and padded off.

Admiral looked back at Shaggy with an annoyed expression, "Anyway, Miss Lily discussed my issues with Dr. Mike and decided she might be able to help me. I went with her and Shaggy into her car, and we arrived here. Everyone came running to meet me, which was alarming because none of the other dogs were friendly where I came from. Miss Lily started hollering, 'Back up.' Then everyone backed up, and I could see all their happy faces. They weren't trying to be mean to me; they were friendly and curious. Miss Lily brought me into the house, but I'd never been in a house before and didn't want rubs and kisses. I wouldn't allow myself to be hugged because I'd never been hugged before."

"I'm so sorry to hear that," I gasped. I'd never known a dog who hadn't been hugged before.

Admiral held up his paw, "Shhh... I'm almost done. Miss Lily may not have been able to hold me, but she always made sure I had something soft to lie on, and she would lay with me whenever I was feeling too anxious to sleep. Shaggy and I became friends, and the other dogs adopted me with no hesitation. Eventually, I was able to accept Miss Lily's love and support. I started eating and sleeping normally again. Okay, finished. Anything else?"

I looked up and thought momentarily, "Why do you constantly patrol without a break?"

Admiral shook his head, "All I love must be guarded and kept safe. If something bad happens on my watch, I could lose all of this. I was trained to patrol, and patrolling is my way of thanking Miss Lily for her kindness."

A panting Shaggy returned to the porch, "Are y'all done yet? I need a break."

Admiral turned and started trotting off, "Yes, I believe so."

"How'd it go?" Shaggy asked as he sat down and turned to me.

I looked out at Admiral patrolling, then back at Shaggy, "Okay, I guess. He's so serious."

Shaggy smiled, "I know. That's just who he is. He simply worries too much."

I nodded, "Well, he has been through a lot. Everyone is different and has different experiences. We'd get bored if we were all the same. I just wish he would relax sometimes."

"He does, but only when Miss Lily is alone with him."

I heard Miss Lily's car coming up the driveway, "Oh no! I lost track of time. I've got to go escort her."

Shaggy wagged his tail, "You'd better hurry, then."

I ran off to meet Miss Lily, thanking Shaggy for his help as I left. Reflecting on my talk with Admiral, I realized it wasn't as intense as I thought it would be. It was nice of Shaggy to help me out. I'm going to start helping Admiral patrol. Patrolling is a big responsibility for one dog to handle, and maybe if I help, Admiral can relax more often. This got me thinking. We should help anybody and everybody we can because that would help spread happiness.

CHAPTER 8

SCRUFFY

One day Shaggy and I were playing in the backyard, racing each other around the lawn when we heard a strange noise. We started sniffing along the fence, which runs along the alleyway at the rear of Miss Lily's property. We looked and looked, but didn't see anything, so we returned to playing. Suddenly Shaggy sat down.

"I saw something over there," Shaggy pointed his nose toward some tall grass in the alley.

I sat next to him, and we both stayed quiet for a minute and watched and listened. "I hear something," I said as I got up and walked toward the fence.

"Me, too," Shaggy cautiously walked up next to me, his nose twitching, trying to smell what it was. "There it is!"

We saw it. It was a teensy, tiny kitten. Its tongue was hanging out as it panted, and it seemed to have trouble walking. "Stay here, Shaggy, and I'll get Miss Lily."

I ran to the house as fast as I could and scooted through the doggy door. "Miss Lily, Miss Lily," I barked as loud as I could.

Miss Lily came out of the kitchen, wiping her hands on a towel. "What's the matter, Copper? Is someone hurt?"

Miss Lily was in her socks, so I kept running around her while she sat in a chair and put on her tennies. "Hurry, hurry," I pleaded, nipping at her pant leg.

"Copper, what's wrong with you? I'm hurrying as fast as I can."

We ran outside and up to Shaggy. Miss Lily crouched down next to him. "What's the matter, boy? Are you hurt?"

Shaggy just sat still, staring toward the fence.

Miss Lily looked in the direction he was looking. "I don't see anything; what's all the fuss about?"

Right then, a tiny squeak came from the kitten. Miss Lily got closer to the fence. "It's just a baby." She reached through the fence and tried to pick the kitten up, but it got to its feet and stumbled out of reach. Miss Lily stood up and ran back into the house. Shaggy and I watched her, confused about why she had left. But she came right back with a can of wonderful-smelling cat food. She pushed the can through the fence. But the kitten just lay down in the grass and stopped moving.

Miss Lily stood up and looked at the fence for a minute, then started climbing over it. It's one of those wire fences Miss Lily calls "chain-link." All I know is that it has spiky things on the top to keep us animals from trying to jump over it. Miss Lily climbed to the top and jumped off the other side. She picked the little kitten up and put him in her mouth like a mommy cat! Sometimes, I think Miss Lily forgets she's a human. She started climbing back over the fence, but her pants got caught on the top spiky things causing her to fall into the grass in our yard. The kitten was safe, but Miss Lily was all scratched up and bruised, and her pants were torn. She got up, took the kitten into her hands, and looked it over. Then she held it close to her chest as she limped back to the house.

Shaggy and I followed her back into the kitchen and watched as she gave the kitten some water with a dropper like she used to give us medicine. Then she took a warm wet cloth and washed the kitten all over very carefully. When the kitten was clean and not panting anymore, she gave it the cat food. You should have seen that kitten eat. He had no manners at all. He got food everywhere and all over himself. He would growl and swipe his claws at anyone who came close to him. Finally, Miss Lily had to take the food away.

"I don't want him to get a tummy ache," she said as the kitten swiped his paw at her. She picked him up and examined him again. His long grey fur was matted around his face and ears from cat food stuck in it. "I think Scruffy would be a good name for you."

Scruffy is now half-grown. He is a silly cat who likes to sleep with Peanut because she licks him and keeps his fur clean. Scruffy has a funny walk because one of his back legs is crooked, but that doesn't stop him from racing around the house. He likes to hide under the couch, and when no one is looking, he runs out and slaps them with his paws. He is one different kitty, but I think as he grows up, he will learn to be a good boy like the rest of us.

Miss Lily sure has a good heart, especially for us animals. Wouldn't it be nice if everyone had a good heart like that?

CHAPTER 9

PEANUT

I was feeling as gloomy as the sky outside. Water had been coming from the sky for several days. Everything was wet, the kind of wet where you only went outside long enough to do your business and then hurried back into the house to shake it all off. The others were feeling it, too. No one was playing. The cats, except for Shadow, who was in her room, were all snuggled up on Miss Lily's bed. Shaggy was asleep in front of the door to the kitchen, Bella was lying under the kitchen table at Miss Lily's feet, and even Admiral was in the house. Although his patrolling was limited, Admiral still paced from room to room, ensuring we were all safe and there were no intruders.

Miss Lily was sitting at the table with piles of papers around her; she calls them her "bills," which is weird because the man who helps her fix the fences and other things around here is also called Bill, and he never brings stacks of paper when he comes only his tools and some tasty snacks for us. Humans are strange sometimes.

I was curled up in the corner of the couch with my head on my paws and thinking of my Amber. Anytime I felt low-spirited, my thoughts were always of Amber and how much I missed her. Just as I sighed a big sigh, Peanut came up to me.

She stood up on her hind legs and wagged her little bit of a tail. "What's the matter, Copper?"

"I don't know. I guess it's the greyness. It makes me want my Amber."

"What if we play tag? That might cheer you up." Her tail wagged even harder.

"I don't think so. I don't feel like running through the house. Besides, it would probably bother everyone else."

Peanut jumped up onto the couch. "You're probably right. Then, can I curl up with you? I don't have as much fur as you do, and I'm cold. I thought running might warm me up."

"Of course, you can curl up with me, but my mood might rub off on you."

Peanut snuggled against me and giggled, "Copper, you're just being silly. How can a mood rub off of someone?"

I raised my head and smiled at her, "I guess that is a little silly. Peanut, why are you always so cheerful? You are the smallest dog I've ever seen, yet you seem to have the biggest heart."

"I guess I have learned that no matter how bad things seem, there's always happiness if you look for it."

"How did you learn that?" I stopped and thought for a minute. "Peanut, I don't know your story or how

71

you came to live with Miss Lily. Maybe if you tell me, it might cheer me up."

"There's not much to tell. But if it helps make you feel better, I'd be happy to." Peanut snuggled up closer and put her head across my leg. "I was born in a place where there were lots of other dogs. All the dogs were in little wire pens. My momma had me and my three brothers in the pen. There was a blanket for us to lay on, but the rest was made of twisted wire stuff with holes between the wires." Peanut stopped for a second, thinking. "Copper, do you remember the coop Miss Lily made for those chickens she kept for Dr. Mike last summer? Our pen was made of the same kind of wire, and it was up off the ground, so if we tried to walk on it, our feet would fall through the holes."

"Why would it be up like that?" I was puzzled at the idea of dogs being kept high off the ground.

Peanut shrugged, "I'm not sure. All I remember is when we went potty, it fell through the wires and piled up on the floor, and then a boy came in every day and sprayed water on the floor with a hose and washed it all away. Sometimes he got in a hurry and sprayed water on us, too."

"That must have been scary."

"It was all we knew. We were in a big building, and there were many cages with dogs in every one. The cages were lined up in rows on both sides of the room. There was a momma dog with new pups on each side of us. If we got too close to them, the momma would growl and snap at us, and our momma would growl and snap back.

"Sometimes one of the dogs would start barking, and pretty soon, others would join in, and it would get so loud it would hurt my ears. When we were old enough to leave our momma, the hose boy and the man who put food and water in our cage came and took us out. He put my brothers in little boxes and told the boy to put them in a truck. I remember him saying, 'These will bring top dollar.'

"Then the man took me and said, 'This one's tail is too short, but it's a female, so we'll keep her.'

"He put me in another cage at the end of the row my momma was in. I remember being scared because I was all alone. I guess I was crying a lot, too. A white dog with knotted curly hair was in the cage next to me. She started talking to me, trying to calm me down.

'I know how you feel. I've been there, too. Come over by me,' she said. 'I'll keep you company.'

"So, I moved closer to her. I could feel her warmth through the wires. Then she said. 'It will be all right; you'll get used to it. When you're old enough, you'll have your own pups. You'll learn to raise them until they are old enough to leave, and then you'll have some more. It just goes that way, day after day, year after year.'

'But what if I don't want to have pups?' I asked. I was still too young to even think about having my own puppies.

'It doesn't matter what you want; it's what you were born to do. The man feeds us, and we give him puppies. That's how it works.'

'You don't have puppies with you. Why is that?'

'I will soon. I'm about three weeks away from having my next ones. They will be my seventh litter.'

'Doesn't it make you sad when your babies are taken away?'

'Yes, at first it does. Especially when I am still full of milk, and it hurts me. But that goes away in a few days, and the man lets me rest for a little while. When I get to rest, that makes me happy.'"

Peanut sighed. "White dog was very nice to me. She taught me lots of things in the short time I knew her. I think if I'd stayed there, she and I would have been good friends."

"What happened? How did you leave? What happened to White Dog?" Peanut had my attention, and I wanted to know more.

"One day, more people than I'd ever seen came into our room. They all seemed so sad. They approached each of our cages and looked at us, talking in low voices. One by one, the people took the dogs out of the cages. We were put into new cages with solid bottoms, tops, and sides. They had open bars on the ends so that we could see out. Inside there were thick, soft blankets we could snuggle down into. These new cages were put into a big truck, and we rode in there to a new place. At the new place, I was examined by a veterinarian, bathed, given shots, and treated for fleas. I had an operation a few days later, so I couldn't have puppies. I wasn't used to being touched by people. I was so scared; I shook all over, but I just kept remembering something White Dog told me."

"What was that?" I asked.

"That no matter how bad things seemed, they would get better. She was right. After the vet was done with me, I was put back into the cage, but only for a little while because a lady came and took me to her house, and before you ask, it wasn't Miss Lily. Her name was Polly. Polly fostered some of the other dogs I arrived with, too."

I raised my head and looked at Peanut. "Wait...what's a foster? Why did she take you and not keep you?"

Peanut sat up. "From what I understand, a foster is a human who takes in dogs with no homes and takes care of them like they were her own until a real home can be found. If the dog needs help with something, she will teach it, so the dog can be a good dog when his real home is found."

"I'm still confused," I said.

"Let's see. How do I explain this? All of us who came from the big room, Polly called it a "puppy mill," were not house trained. We didn't know how to do anything. She taught us manners, she taught us to potty outside, and she taught us how to play with each other.

She taught us there was more to life than living in a little wire cage and having puppies. It was still frightening for me, but Polly was gentle and patient. I didn't know what to do the first time she put me on the grass so I could potty. I'd never been on grass before. I was so surprised at the feeling on my paws. The grass was soft and prickly all at the same time. I kept lifting my feet one by one and looking at them. I thought something was crawling on them. But Polly softly stroked my back, talked to me, and told me it would be okay. It didn't take me long to figure it out, and pretty soon, I was running and playing on the grass. Polly gave me confidence and the ability to move forward."

"Wow, Polly does seem special. So why didn't you stay with her?"

"I wanted to. But then I thought if I stayed, that would mean another dog might not know Polly's kindness and love, and they might not find their own home because I was being selfish. I was actually at Polly's longer than I should have been. For some reason, nobody wanted to adopt me. But I wasn't the only one having trouble finding a new family; some of the older momma dogs also had longer stays. It seemed like the little puppies were the first to find homes. I was still kind of a puppy, but I was a bit older than some. I was glad of that, though, because it meant I got to stay with Polly longer.

"Then, one day, Polly brought a new dog home. It was White Dog! I didn't know her at first because she was so pretty. Her hair had all been cut off and combed out. The best thing was that now I could help her as she'd helped me. She was scared at first, too, but I kept reminding her what she always told me, that things would get better. We were together for a few weeks, and she quickly learned her manners.

"One afternoon, Polly had some of us out in the grass when a lady came to visit and look at us. Polly told her I was having trouble finding a home. The lady picked me up and said she would love to help out. She gave me time to say goodbye to White Dog and put me in a soft carrier. We had a long ride, and she talked to me the entire time. She had me wagging my little tail all the way."

"It was Miss Lily!" I interrupted.

Peanut smiled and nodded her head, "It was Miss Lily. After I was here for a few days and made friends with the others, Miss Lily said I was a joy to have around and told me I could stay with her as long as I wanted. And that's why I am always cheerful. I know I have nothing to be afraid of here. I know I will always have a soft bed and good food, and friends to be with. I have also learned that you can give happiness to others without losing it for yourself."

"You're right, Peanut. Being happy and cheerful makes life so much easier for everybody. Thank you for telling me your story; even if you didn't feel you had much to say, you told me so much. Thanks to you, I am in a better mood now. Want to play tag?"

CHAPTER 10

AMETHYST

Recently, I learned all about being different. Some of us are more different than others. For instance, Peanut is tiny while I am big. Peanut's fur is short, while mine is long. She is black and brown, and I'm all red. We are much different dogs, and yet we are excellent friends. The same with Shaggy. Shaggy is big like me, but he is a light tan color, and his fur is curly, while mine is straight.

On the other hand, cats are totally different creatures, not just because they're different animals from dogs, but because they have such strange ways of doing things. A good example is Amethyst.

When Miss Lily brought Amethyst home, she was in a special cat carrier. It wasn't like the typical soft carrier Miss Lily usually used, but it was more like a heavy, thick box with little holes on the side so the cat could see out and breathe.

When Miss Lily came into the house, she asked us to be quiet and calm. "Amethyst is not having a good day. She's upset about coming here, but no one else will take her because she doesn't like people much."

When Miss Lily tried to take Amethyst out of the carrier, that cat came out with the wildest noise I've ever heard. She was quick and wriggled out of Miss

Lily's hands and went straight up Miss Lily, digging her sharp claws into Miss Lily's face. Poor Miss Lily was left with scratches all over her arms and face. And then Amethyst took off running frantically through the house. She headed down the hallway, and I thought for sure she was headed for the cat room. But instead, she ran into the guest room! The guest room is always off-limits for all of us animals. But I guess Miss Lily left the door open just enough that the cat could dart through it. She ran in and went straight under the bed. And that's where she stayed.

Amethyst was a pretty cat. She was a light cream color with purple-grey tips on her ears, feet, nose, and tail. Her dark blue eyes always stayed in a tight squint, making her look really mean.

Miss Lily followed the cat into the guest room and looked under the bed to see if she could get Amethyst out from under it, but she just decided to let the cat stay right where she was. Miss Lily came out of the room and closed the door behind her. "I think it is best to give her space. I'll bring her food, water, and a litter box in a little while."

For several days, Miss Lily would enter the guest room and close the door behind her. I would lay out in the hallway listening for any trouble, but Miss Lily would spend a long time being extremely quiet. Finally, Miss Lily decided that Amethyst needed to see out.

As Miss Lily put up a gate, like the one she has at the door to the kitchen, she said, "Amethyst needs to know what is going on in the house. She needs to get used to seeing and hearing the rest of you. Maybe that will help her come out of her shell."

The gate was short enough I could jump over it, but I respected that Miss Lily didn't want us in there and needed Amethyst to feel safe. But every time somebody walked by that gate, the most horrible, growling roar would come out from under that bed and fill the whole house with a life-threatening warning. It was enough to make everybody shudder and tip-toe past that doorway. But Miss Lily kept going into that room. She would sit on the floor near the bed; sometimes, she would stay quiet, and other times she would talk to Amethyst calm-ly. I sat quite still outside the gate and watched.

One day, Amethyst emerged from under the bed and sniffed Miss Lily. I watched her closely because I was afraid she would claw Miss Lily up like before, but she didn't. She only sniffed Miss Lily all over. Eventually, she curled up on the floor near Miss Lily but would not get in her lap. I was surprised she even got that close to being a relaxed cat. But each day, Amethyst got a little better and a little braver. And a little less mean. But she never came out of the room. Even when the gate was open, although the rest of us did not go inside because we were afraid we'd get clawed, she would not come out.

One day, there was a knock on the front door, and when Miss Lily answered, a lady and a boy stood on the front porch.

"I was told you have cats available for adoption," the lady said. "I would like to find a friend for my son. He has developmental disabilities, and we've been looking for the right pet for him. He seems to like cats the most."

Miss Lily smiled at the lady and said, "Yes, I have several kittens he might like. Please come in."

When the boy came into the house, I saw he was different. He didn't talk; he only made funny noises. I thought all humans could talk, but I keep learning new things about them all the time. He was a big boy, almost a full-grown human. I was confused because he acted like a small boy. He also had the biggest smile when Miss Lily brought out the little kittens and showed them to the lady and the boy.

They looked at all the kitties available for adoption from Miss Lily's Rescue, but it seemed the boy couldn't decide on any of them. Then, while the lady and Miss Lily were talking, the boy wandered down the hallway toward the guest room. He stopped as he looked in and then sat on the floor outside the gate. The next thing that happened was pretty unbelievable. Amethyst walked up to the gate and began sniffing him, meowing quietly. Her eyes softened, and I could see how blue they truly were.

Miss Lily took notice and watched for a minute, "If you want to go in, just open the gate," she told him.

His mother said, "Go ahead; it's all right. The lady said you can go in."

The boy opened the gate, entered the room, and sat on the edge of the bed. I held my breath, expecting the worst, when Amethyst hopped up on the bed and rubbed her head against the boy's side. He made giggling noises as she curled up in his lap. Nobody could believe it, not even Miss Lily. And then Amethyst began purring! The loud and continuous hum was the first time anyone had heard her purr.

Miss Lily began explaining to the lady about Amethyst's issues, "Amethyst is an extremely wild cat. She hasn't shown anything but contempt for me or any of the animals since she's been here. I am not only surprised at how she's taken to your son; I'm stunned. I just want you to be aware of this information."

As they talked, Miss Lily kept an eye on Amethyst and pretended to ignore what was happening. The boy picked Amethyst up. No one had picked her up since she'd clawed Miss Lily so badly. But Amethyst only snuggled her head against the boy. It was like instant love. I couldn't believe what I was seeing. But Amethyst was happy. That's the happiest I've ever seen a cat. Finally, the boy carried Amethyst out of the guest room and over to his mother. He kept pointing at the cat and making noises.

His mother smiled and said, "We would like this cat. Maybe it's because my son is different. The cat can tell he needs love like she needs love. He has no friends. And she is what he needs."

And so they left, with the boy carrying Amethyst and Amethyst snuggled up against his shirt.

I never got Amethyst's story or found out where she came from. But Amethyst made her own story here at Miss Lily's Rescue. Because of her, I've discovered that being different is one of the things we all have in common. Being different and accepting our differences will help us share the love with everybody.

CHAPTER 11

LIZZYBET

Peanut experienced something awful this week, and since I learned that sharing bad things can make you feel better, I decided to talk to her; actually, I did more listening than talking. And I wanted to share it with you. It is a bit sad, so prepare yourself.

Peanut was sitting on the porch, staring out into the distance. I was out lying in the grass and looked over and saw the sad look on her face, which was strange because Peanut is always such a happy dog. Peanut looked down, and I thought she might cry.

I stood and walked over to her. "Peanut, are you okay?"

Peanut sniffed back a tear, "Kind of."

I sat beside her and gently put my paw on her shoulder. "You don't sound okay."

A single tear splashed down on the floor. "I know," she whimpered.

I nudged her with my nose. "It helps to talk about things. I'm a pretty good listener; I've been practicing." More tears leaked from Peanut's eyes, so I kissed some of them away. "I don't like to see you sad. What's wrong?"

Peanut sniffed back her tears and cleared her throat, "Oh, Copper, you know Lizzybet?"

I looked at her, a bit puzzled. "Of course, she's your favorite Teddy bear. You take her every…." I stopped because that's when I realized something terrible had happened. I swallowed hard, "Oh no…."

Peanut started sobbing.

I didn't know what to say. So, I did the only thing I knew…I licked her face.

Peanut took a deep breath. "Bella and I were in the living room waiting for Miss Lily to come home. And…and…and…." Peanut let out a mournful sob. "And when we heard Miss Lily drive up, we got so excited. Bella ran into Miss Lily's room, and I thought she was going to get one of her toys like she always does, but…but…." Peanut lay down in her river of tears and cried even more.

I nuzzled her, trying to comfort her. "She grabbed Lizzybet, didn't she?"

Peanut miserably howled, "YESSS!"

I didn't know what to say. It hurt my heart to see her so sad. Peanut took a couple of deep breaths and continued. "Bella grabbed Lizzybet, ripped off her arm, and pulled out some fluff. I begged her to stop. It was like she couldn't even hear me. Then she grabbed Lizzybet's ear and ripped the top of her head open. I was stunned. All I could do was cry as I watched her pull out and throw Lizzybet's fluff everywhere. There was fluff flying like snow. I was frozen by the horror and shock of what was happening. When Miss Lily came into the house, I think she heard Bella's happy yips, so she came into the bedroom. She told Bella 'NO,' took Lizzybet from her, and sent her outside. Then Miss Lily let me out because I couldn't bear the sight. There was so much fluff…." Peanut wailed. "It was too late. I know it. Lizzybet isn't going to…"

Just then, Miss Lily opened the door and stepped out on the porch. She walked over to where Peanut and I were sitting. Peanut sat up with a wet face and more tears in her eyes. Miss Lily tenderly wiped the tears from Peanut's face. "It's going to be okay. I think I can fix Lizzybet. Why don't you come inside?"

Peanut looked up at me, "Copper, will you come too?"

I nodded, and we all went inside. Peanut and I sat in the living room, watching Miss Lily gather a needle, thread, and the pieces of Lizzybet's fluff. Peanut trembled at the sight, and I put my paw on hers to help her steady herself. She swallowed hard as Miss Lily sat down with poor Lizzybet. Peanut winced every time the needle pierced Lizzybet's fur, every time Miss Lily pushed in more fluff. She was so heartbroken and worried that she couldn't bear to watch the whole process, so she went to Miss Lily's room and cried softly. It was hard to see Peanut like that. I joined her in Miss Lily's room and snuggled with her while we waited.

I thought about something Peanut has told me many times. "Peanut, you know how you always say, 'I have learned that no matter how bad things seem, there's always happiness if you look for it?' I think this is one of those times. You'll see."

It seemed like forever, but finally, Miss Lily called Peanut. Peanut went into the living room, still shaking because she was very nervous. She was scared for Lizzybet. She wasn't sure her special friend would make it through the surgery.

When Miss Lily held up Lizzybet, Peanut lit up and started dancing. Her little tail wagged so hard that her whole body wiggled. She grabbed Lizzybet from Miss Lily, danced with her, loved her, and groomed her. "MISS LILY SAVED LIZZYBET! '" Peanut shrieked.

Miss Lily smiled sympathetically, "I'm sorry I couldn't make Lizzybet perfect."

Peanut beamed back at Miss Lily. "Lizzybet doesn't have to be perfect. She's my friend. It's okay that she looks different. Looks don't matter. It's the love that we share that matters, not her looks. I love Lizzybet no matter what."

When I heard Peanut say that, my heart melted. She is absolutely right. It's not what we look like; it is the love we share that matters.

CHAPTER 12

RUSTY

I was barely awake when I heard Miss Lily leave the house. Curious, I jumped up on the couch to look out the big window and watch for her return; I was worried she'd be gone a long time and had forgotten to feed us. The birds who lived in the big tree in the yard were also beginning to wake. I watched as they shook their feathers and hopped down into the grass, looking for their breakfast. Finally, I saw Miss Lily's car come up the road.

When she entered the house, Miss Lily had another long-haired red dog with her. He was smaller than me, his ears were long, and while the rest of his fur was straight like mine, the fur on his ears formed waves across them.

The strangest thing about him was the cage on his face. I'd never seen anything like this before and was curious about it. I walked over to him and began sniffing all the usual places to introduce myself and learn about him. He drew back from me, so I thought he might be afraid. I backed away and gave him time to settle in and get to know the house and some of the rules. When I saw him lying on the floor by the couch, I thought it was time to officially introduce myself and maybe find out why he had this face-cage thing.

"Hi, my name is Copper," I said as I wagged my tail in greeting.

He looked up at me. "I'm Rusty," he sighed and laid his head back on his paws.

"You miss your family, don't you? I know the feeling, but if they can be found, Miss Lily will find them."

"No, it's not that at all. This is the fourth house I've been to. It seems no one wants me because I bite people. That's why I have to wear this awful muzzle."

"A muzzle? I've worn a muzzle before, but not like that one." I sniffed it, but it just smelled like Shaggy's rubber ball.

"This one is for biters. I have to wear it all the time. It's made so I can eat and drink with it on."

"That's terrible. But why do you bite? I've never bit anyone except for a few nasty fleas that bit me first."

"I don't mean to bite, but people always touch my ears and hurt me, so I just react without thinking. That's why I must wear this muzzle, but it hurts, too." Rusty gave a quiet groan.

"Why does it hurt?"

"Do you see how the straps that hold it on go behind my ears? That puts pressure on them and keeps them sore."

"I'm not sure I quite understand, but I'm not exactly experienced," I said, trying to lighten his mood. "You said this is your fourth house; you are fairly young to have been moved around like that. Would you tell me about the others?"

"At first, I was with a family who took good care of me most of the time. And then, one day, my ears started bothering me; they burned down deep inside. I was still a pup, so I cried a lot, but they didn't notice. One afternoon, my human mama started brushing my ears, and the more she brushed, the more they hurt. I tried to pull away from her, but she kept holding me down and brushing and brushing; I finally couldn't take it anymore, so I bit her hand.

"She screamed at me and slapped me across the head. I was taken to the animal shelter right after that. I felt terrible that I'd bitten her, but she would not leave my ears alone.

"I was at the shelter for some time when I was adopted by a family with a small boy. I wasn't with them for long because I bit him on the leg the first time the boy pulled on my ears. I warned him with a loud growl, but he didn't stop. They didn't take me back to the shelter like I thought they would. Instead, they gave me to a young man who lived alone.

"Things were going well; he seemed to understand that I didn't want my ears touched. Then one night, he had a lot of people in his house. He called it a party. All the people seemed to like me and paid a great deal of attention to me. I got tired and went into the bedroom for some quiet when a lady came in to take me back out to where everyone was. That's when she grabbed my ears, pulled them back, and lifted me up by them. I let out a scream and bit her in the mouth. She threw me across the room. My human came in and yelled at me, then threw me out into the backyard. I cried all night because my ears hurt so much. The next day, he put this muzzle on me. He made me stay out in the yard and didn't come to see me except when he brought me food. I decided I didn't like him all that much, so I refused to go to him when he called me. He told me I was useless and not worth keeping around. This morning he came out to the yard and said he was taking me to the dog park. I was excited to go to the park because I could run and play with other dogs. I jumped in his car, happy to get out of that yard for a while. When we got there, he took me straight over to a lady who was waiting for us."

"Miss Lily?" I asked.

"Oh, is that her name? Anyway, she let me run and play while she talked to my human. Then I saw him get back into his car and leave. I was upset that I was being given away again, but then I remembered I would only have to stay in his backyard, so maybe this won't be so bad." Rusty squinted his eyes closed, and I could see his pain.

Miss Lily came into the room and approached us. "Copper, I see you are making friends with our new Cocker Spaniel. This poor guy has a bad reputation, but

I'm hoping we can figure out his issues and maybe make him a better companion."

I stood up and wagged my tail but kept between her and Rusty. Every time she tried to get close to him, I moved to block her.

"Copper, what are you doing? I can't check him out if you're in the way."

I sat down again and put my back paw in my ear like I was trying to dig something out of it.

"Is there something wrong with your ear, Copper? Here, let me look at it."

I stood up and backed away from her. Then I looked over at Rusty.

"Come here, Copper, let me see your ear." Miss Lily reached out to me, but I just kept backing away, this time shaking my head hard.

"Copper, what's wrong!" Miss Lily's frustration was evident in her voice.

I had another idea about how to get Miss Lily to understand. I stepped forward and put my paw on Rusty's back, being careful not to get too close to his ears.

Miss Lily sat back on her heels and watched me. Then she looked down at Rusty, who was lying remarkably still. "Are you trying to tell me something is wrong with Rusty?"

I backed away from Rusty and wagged my tail.

"Is it his ears?"

I wagged my tail even harder.

Miss Lily stood up. "I'll call Dr. Mike and see if he has any ideas. Rusty needs to be checked out anyway if he's going to stay here."

She disappeared into the kitchen, where she is always leaving her little calling box. Soon she returned with a leash in her hand.

"Come on, Rusty, Dr. Mike would like to meet you." She clipped the leash to Rusty's collar, and he followed her out to her car.

It seemed like a long time before I heard Miss Lily's car return to the yard. I jumped up on the couch, looked out the big window, and watched Miss Lily lift a sleeping Rusty out of the back seat and carry him into the house. He wasn't wearing his muzzle! I was worried something terrible had happened at Dr. Mike's, so I ran to meet them at the door.

When Miss Lily came in, she placed Rusty on the couch. "He's doing okay, Copper. Dr. Mike had to make Rusty sleepy so he could look in his ears. He found a bad infection deep down in Rusty's ears and said it had been there for a long time. He also said the infection makes Rusty's ears painful, and that's probably why he bites. He gave Rusty an injection to fight the infection and put some ointment in his ears. I must put cream in his ears daily until the infection is gone. I'll have to muzzle him for that, but Dr. Mike gave me a soft one with no straps. We'll see how he does with it." She reached down and stroked my head. "Copper, I'm proud of you. You are smart and a good boy for telling me about Rusty."

I wagged my tail and licked the back of her hand, then sat by the couch to keep an eye on Rusty. When he woke up, he looked at me and smiled a little doggy smile. I licked his nose to comfort him.

"What happened? I remember going into the special room with the metal table and meeting Dr. Mike. I remember getting a shot but nothing else." Rusty looked down his nose, "I'm not wearing my muzzle!" He paused… "And my ears don't hurt as much."

"And soon they won't hurt at all," I encouraged him. "Miss Lily said you had a 'fection making your ears hurt. She will have to put stuff in your ears until they are all better, but you'll have to be nice and not bite her. She did say Dr. Mike gave her a new muzzle with no straps."

"Really? No Straps? I think I like that idea." Rusty jumped down off the couch and rubbed his nose against my neck. "Thank you, Copper. No one has understood me, but Miss Lily understood you. I feel better now and look forward to my ears not hurting again."

I happily returned his licks. I saw the others heading for the kitchen. "Are you hungry? It looks like it's time to eat."

"Let's go! I'm ready to meet everybody else."

Sometimes we all need a little help but don't always know who or how to ask for it. That's where a friend can be valuable. A good friend will listen to your problems, and sometimes they will know how to help you or tell somebody knowledgeable to get you the help you need. Trust in your friends and be a trustworthy friend in return.

CHAPTER 13

TOPAZ

Miss Lily brought two big empty boxes into the house and took them to her sleeping room. I followed her to see what she was going to do with them. Topaz was sleeping on Miss Lily's pillow when we entered the room.

Topaz is an orange cat, but his color differs from Old Jake's. Jake is a dark orange color with lighter orange stripes; Topaz is lighter orange with brownish stripes mixed in. But Miss Lily says they are both Tabby cats. I don't know all that much about the different kinds of cats; after all, I'd never met a cat until I came to live here.

Miss Lily put the boxes on the floor in front of where she keeps everything she puts on. Humans are weird that way. They don't have fur like the rest of us, so they must put stuff on to protect their skin. Anyway, she started pulling her coverups out and putting them in the boxes.

When she saw me watching her, Miss Lily said, "I am finally getting around to cleaning my old clothes out of the closet. It's been too long, and I'm running out of room to keep extra blankets and towels for my rescues. I'm going to give these clothes to people who need them."

I didn't fully understand, but whatever she was doing seemed to make her happy. When the first box was full, Miss Lily carried it out to her car, then returned to fill the other one. After she left the room, I noticed Topaz was no longer on the pillow. In fact, he didn't even seem to be in the room. I hadn't seen him leave and didn't know where he might have gone, but thought he might be hiding under the bed for some reason.

I decided to help Miss Lily by checking out all the things she was putting in the box and nosing some of them into place so they fit just right. I forgot all about Topaz.

At dinnertime, when Miss Lily set out our food bowls, dogs on one side of the porch and cats on the other, Topaz's bowl sat untouched. Miss Lily called, "Topaz, here kitty...kitty." But Topaz didn't come.

I hurried and finished my meal, then went looking for him. I could hear Miss Lily calling again as I went back to the sleeping room. I looked under the bed, on the bed, and all around the room. Then I checked in the cat room. Shadow was eating her dinner in her crate like she always did.

"What do you want?" she hissed.

"I was looking for Topaz," I said as I slowly backed out of the room.

"Haven't seen him all day; now go away so I can eat."

"Yes, ma'am."

Miss Lily met me in the hallway. "Copper, are you looking for Topaz too? Good boy."

I wagged my tail in response. Then I remembered I hadn't looked in Miss Lily's potty room. I didn't go in there often because that's where we got washed or had some of our little cuts and scrapes fixed. As I sniffed around the room, I heard the tiniest noise come from the space under the big water bowl. "Topaz, are you in there?"

Silence followed. The little door was closed, but I could smell him.

"Topaz, I know you're in there. Why won't you answer me?"

I heard him sniffle. "I don't want to be thrown out again."

"I don't understand," I said. "Why would you think you're going to be thrown out?"

"Because that's what happened last time."

I could hear the sadness in his voice. I also felt he was scared, too. "Tell me what you are talking about. I still don't understand."

He was quiet for a bit, then began his story in a low voice. "When I was still a kitten, I went to live with three young men in a small house they called an apartment. I think they might have been going to a learning place because there were always lots of books and papers and 'puters lying around the rooms. I had lots of fun with them hiding under their books and running across the springy black letters on their 'puters. They were also good to sleep with and let me curl up against their heads or along their sides. But, shortly before my first birthday, they all began bringing big boxes into the house. I thought the boxes were for me to play in, and I had a good time jumping in and out of them. They shooed me away when they started putting their books and other things into them.

"Then the boys began putting all the boxes into their cars, and soon, the apartment was empty. I was picked up and thought I would get to go for a ride in one of the cars, but I was carried out to the place where the big trash bins were and left on the ground. My feeding and water bowls, some food, and my bed were left there, too. I was confused, so I just sat there and watched as the last car drove away. I waited and waited for someone to come back, but no one did. A few strangers brought big bags and put them in the bins, but no one picked me up or acted like they even saw me. I waited there until a big truck came and lifted the bins, then I was so scared I ran out in front of the truck. A man got out, picked me up, and put me in the truck with him. I cried and cried. I think I cried so much that he thought something was wrong with me, so he left me with a lady at one of his stops. She brought me to Miss Lily. And now Miss Lily is packing up boxes…." Topaz began crying out loud. "I'm not coming out," he wailed.

I felt terrible for Topaz; he seemed so miserable. "Miss Lily's not going anywhere," I tried to soothe him. "She's only cleaning out some of her old stuff to make more room for our stuff."

"Are you sure?" Topaz whimpered.

I had an idea. "Why don't you come out of there and see for yourself? Miss Lily has finished doing what she was doing, and you can see that nothing has changed except for more blankets and towels in the space she cleared out."

Topaz slowly came out from behind the door. I licked him on the head and ruffled the fur on his neck with my nose. "Come on, and I'll show you." He followed me into Miss Lily's sleeping room, and I showed him the new pile of things for us.

Miss Lily came into the room. "There you are, Topaz. Where have you been? Copper, did you find him for me? You're such a good boy." Miss Lily picked Topaz up and held him close, "You've missed your dinner, but I saved it for you. We'll see if you're hungry now."

Topaz purred and rubbed his head against Miss Lily, then looked down at me and said, "Thank you, Copper, for understanding why I was so afraid."

Sometimes we all are afraid. Most of the time, what causes us to be afraid is something we experienced in the past but is not true now. Having someone to help us understand our fears is an essential part of learning not to be afraid and allows us to move forward confidently.

I have learned that transforming your fear into trust will teach you to rise above worry and doubt.

CHAPTER 14

FINAL THOUGHTS

The night was warm, and the dark, clear sky was dotted with twinkling stars. Shaggy and I were lying on our backs in the grass, looking up at them, when I heard Peanut approaching us. I always know when Peanut is coming because the tags on her collar make a particular clinking sound when she trots.

"Copper, what are you guys doing?"

I looked over at her as she sat beside me, "I'm looking for my Amber, and Shaggy is looking for his Ernie."

"I don't understand," Peanut said.

I lifted my paw and pointed toward the sky.

Peanut laughed. "Those are stars."

I gave a short nod and continued to gaze at the night sky. Shaggy rolled over and gave Peanut a meaningful look, "That's where our Rainbow Bridge friends are. When night settles in, they go to their special stars and watch us from there. Each friend gets their own star. That's why there are so many."

Peanut looked up, "Is that where my momma went?"

I smiled thoughtfully, "I'm sure it is. And my best friend, Amber, and Shaggy's Ernie, and everyone who has touched our hearts and had to leave us."

Peanut sat between Shaggy and me and looked up at the shining dots in the sky. "Why can't we go up there to visit?"

I rolled over onto my stomach and sighed, feeling sad and missing my Amber, "because we have too much to look after here."

Peanut rubbed her face on my fur, "That makes me sad. Why can't they come to visit us?"

I looked over and saw a tear running down the side of her nose. I licked the tear off her whiskers. "Because they have special jobs at the Rainbow Bridge now. They gave us their wisdom and love and have taught us to be able to take care of things here until we get our own call to cross the bridge."

Peanut sniffled as Shaggy interrupted, "I miss Ernie. He had the best stories. We traveled all around the city together and met lots of interesting people. Those were good years." Shaggy let out a long sigh and returned his gaze to the sky.

I sat up and placed one toe lightly on Peanut's chest, "Those we love will always be here, in our hearts. Our Rainbow Bridge friends left us with many stories and adventures, love, and wisdom to share. They will never be forgotten as long as the stars shine and we take the time to look for them."

Peanut's face opened up into a smile, then she sat up like she was begging for a cookie, "I think I see my momma's star; it's the bright one right there!" She pointed her paw straight up.

"Of course, her star will be a bright one. The more love someone gives and the bigger their heart, the brighter their star will be." Shaggy explained.

I lifted my paw and pointed at a star, too. "That's my Amber. She loved me a lot. She taught me manners and tricks and how to be a good dog. She always took care of me. On my first night here, when Miss Lily told me about Amber going over the Rainbow Bridge, I didn't fully understand what she meant. I just knew something was wrong when Amber's daddy left me by the side of the road. But I have learned what she was trying to explain to me. Whenever Miss Lily has to put in lots of extra care for the tiny kittens and puppies she brings home to foster, and when one of them is too sick to live, I know they have gone to the Rainbow Bridge. I have seen how sad Miss Lily is at first, but then she says, 'Another one has been chosen to travel to the Bridge where they will be happy and healthy and live forever.' That makes her feel better. And, once I understood, it helped me to miss my Amber a little less because I know she will forever be in my heart."

The moon slowly came out from behind the big tree. It was gigantic and bright and as round as my tennis ball. Peanut pointed at it. "And when Miss Lily has to walk over that Rainbow Bridge, that will be her star because she has the biggest heart of all!"

"Peanut, that's the moon. It's not a real star."

Peanut dropped her paw and hung her head, "Oh, but I want Miss Lily to have the biggest star in the whole sky."

I nudged Peanut with my nose until she turned around, and then I pointed to the brightest star in the whole sky, "Miss Lily once told me that the big star there is the largest one. And guess what it's called…the dog star! I think that one is so big that Miss Lily will even have to share it."

"Who would she share it with?" Peanut looked at me with surprise in her eyes.

"They would be all of the other people who rescue or foster or volunteer their lives to help save lost or hurt or mistreated animals like us. They are the people who have so much love to give that their hearts are as big as Miss Lily's."

"That's perfect, Copper. But let's hope Miss Lily doesn't go there for a long, long time."

We all nodded in agreement, then rolled onto our backs, looked back up at the stars, and told each other stories until bedtime.

We may have friends or family who are no longer with us, but remember; they are always with us in our hearts. Share the love, knowledge, and stories they left us with. Remember the lessons they taught, like the ones I learned from my friends at the rescue. Above all, be kind to those who can't speak for themselves, whether an animal or a person. Because all any of us wants is to love and be loved.

I'm Copper, and I love you.

COPPER'S FAVORITE COOKIES

Ingredients:

2 Cups old-fashioned oats

2 Over-ripe bananas

½ Cup peanut butter (natural or low sugar is best)

Preheat the oven to 300f.

Place the oats into a food processor or blender and blend until powdered.

Peel the bananas and drop them into the oat powder; add the peanut butter and blend until a sticky dough forms.

Using oat flour, lightly dust the surface where you will roll out the dough. Roll out to about ½" thick.

Cut out the dough using cookie cutters in your favorite shape, and place on a parchment-lined cookie sheet.

Bake for 25 to 30 minutes.

Remove from oven and let cool for 5 minutes, then transfer to cooling racks. Cookies will firm up as they cool.

Store in your pup's favorite treat jar.

MISS LILY'S KITTY TREATS

Tuna Cookies

Ingredients:

1¼ Cups canned tuna

1 egg

2 Cups whole wheat flour

Preheat the oven to 350f

Put the tuna and the egg into a blender and pulse until blended.

Place this mixture into a bowl and stir in the flour until a dough forms. If it's too dry, add water a teaspoonful at a time. The dough should be workable but not too sticky.

Roll out on a lightly floured surface to about ½" thick. Using cookie cutters, cut into shapes of your choice. Fish shapes are really cute!

Place on a parchment-lined cookie or baking sheet and bake for about 20 minutes (ovens will vary).

Cool completely before serving.

Store in zipper-lock bags and keep in the refrigerator for freshness.

A LAST WORD FROM COPPER

ADOPT, DON'T SHOP

If you can't adopt, **FOSTER**

If you can't foster, **VOLUNTEER**

If you can't volunteer, **DONATE**

If you can't donate, **EDUCATE**

Anyone can do something to help save lives!

Be a part of something bigger than you, and you will be happier and healthier for it.

Also, and this is very important, **SPAY or NEUTER** your pets to help control the pet population.

Have your pets **MICROCHIPPED,** too, because should they get lost, they will have identification that can't be lost, removed, or become impossible to read.

Printed in the USA
CPSIA information can be obtained
at www.ICGtesting.com
BVHW041149070823
668302BV00002B/12

9 780997 927177